My Family

Paul Humphrey

Photography by Chris Fairclough

FRANKLIN WATTS
LONDON·SYDNEY

First published in 2005 by
Franklin Watts
96 Leonard Street
London EC2A 4XD

Franklin Watts Australia
Level 17/207 Kent Street
Sydney NSW 2000

ISBN 0 7496 6171 2 (hbk)
ISBN 0 7496 6183 6 (pbk)

Dewey classification number 306.85

A CIP catalogue record for this book is available
from the British Library.

Planning and production by Discovery Books Limited
Editor: Rachel Tisdale
Designer: Ian Winton
Photography: Chris Fairclough
Series advisors: Diana Bentley MA and Dee Reid MA,
Fellows of Oxford Brookes University

The author, packager and publisher would like to thank the
following people for their participation in this book: Michael,
Linda and Jeremy Bloomfield and family; Julie and Kevin
Morris and family; Megan Merten-Jones.

Printed in China

Contents

My name is Michael 4

My mum and dad 6

My sister and brother 8

Playing together 10

Arguing 12

Granny and grandad 14

My uncles and aunts 16

My cousins 18

Cousins far away 20

I love my family 22

Word bank 24

My name is Michael and this is my family.

5

My dad works in an office.

My mum runs
a shop.

I've got a big sister
and a little brother.

Sometimes
we play
together.

Sometimes
we argue.

It's my turn now!

My granny and grandad often come to stay.

15

I've got lots of uncles, aunties and cousins.

Some of my cousins live nearby.

Some of my cousins
live a long way away.

22

I love my family.

Word bank

Look back for these words and pictures.

Aunties

Brother

Cousins

Dad

Grandad

Granny

Mum

Sister

Uncles

24